The Constitution
of the
United States

Other titles in The Constitution and the United States Government *series:*

The President and the Executive Branch:
How Our Nation is Governed
ISBN: 978-0-7660-4063-2

The United States Congress and the Legislative Branch:
How the Senate and House of Representatives Create Our Laws
ISBN: 978-0-7660-4066-3

The Supreme Court and the Judicial Branch:
How the Federal Courts Interpret Our Laws
ISBN: 978-0-7660-4065-6

The Security Agencies of the United States:
How the CIA, FBI, NSA and Homeland Security Keep Us Safe
ISBN: 978-0-7660-4064-9

The Constitution and the United States Government

THE CONSTITUTION
OF THE
UNITED STATES

Karen Judson

Enslow Publishers, Inc.
40 Industrial Road
Box 398
Berkeley Heights, NJ 07922
USA

http://www.enslow.com

Original edition published as *The Constitution of the United States* in 1996.

Library of Congress Cataloging-in-Publication Data

Judson, Karen, 1941-
    The Constitution of the United States: its history, Bill of Rights, and amendments/Karen Judson.—[Rev. ed.]
        p. cm.—(Constitution and the United States government)
    Previous ed.: published c1996.
    Includes bibliographical references and index.
    ISBN 978-0-7660-4067-0 (alk. paper)
    1. Constitutional history—United States.
I. Title.
KF4541.J83 2012
342.7302'9—dc23

                                        2011030976

    Future editions
    Paperback ISBN 978-1-4644-0173-2
    ePUB ISBN 978-1-4645-1080-9
    PDF ISBN 978-1-4646-1080-6

Printed in the United States of America.

032012 Lake Book Manufacturing, Inc., Melrose Park, IL

10 9 8 7 6 5 4 3 2 1

To Our Readers: We have done our best to make sure all Internet addresses in this book were active and appropriate when we went to press. However, the author and the publisher have no control over and assume no liability for the material available on those Internet sites or on other Web sites they may link to. Any comments or suggestions can be sent by e-mail to comments@enslow.com or to the address on the back cover.

✿ Enslow Publishers, Inc., is committed to printing our books on recycled paper. The paper in every book contains 10% to 30% post-consumer waste (PCW). The cover board on the outside of each book contains 100% PCW. Our goal is to do our part to help young people and the environment too!

Photo Credits: Architect of the Capitol, p. 39; ©Artville, pp. 63, 77; ©Clipart.com, p. 26; Courtesy of U.S. Army, p. 47; ©Enslow Publishers, Inc., p. 43; Library of Congress, pp. 11, 13, 30, 35; National Archives and Records Administration, pp. 57, 71; ©2011 Photos.com, a division of Getty Images. All rights reserved., pp. 17, 20, 68, 70; Shutterstock.com, pp. 9, 23, 33, 65; Supplied by Fort Dodge, Iowa, Police Department, p. 74; U.S. Supreme Court, p. 46.

Cover Illustration:
United States Park Service

CONTENTS

1 Fifty-Five Founding Fathers 7

2 Creating a Constitution 16

3 Resolving Major Issues 41

4 The Bill of Rights 55

5 It's a Free Country 61

Appendix A: The Signers 79

Appendix B: Preamble to the 90
United States Constitution

Appendix C: The Bill of Rights 91

Glossary 94

Chapter Notes 97

Further Reading 100

Internet Addresses 101

Index 102

1

Fifty-Five Founding Fathers

By mid-May of 1787, summer had already arrived in Philadelphia, Pennsylvania. The heat and humidity were intense. Mosquitoes and biting black flies swarmed everywhere.

In 1787, Philadelphia was the largest city in America, with a population of 40,000. The eastern seaboard city had been chosen to host the nation's first Constitutional Convention. The convention was scheduled to begin May 14. Duly chosen delegates were to arrive from twelve of the thirteen states.

The thirteen states in existence in 1787 were Connecticut, Delaware, Georgia, Maryland, Massachusetts, New Hampshire, New Jersey, New York, North and South Carolina, Pennsylvania, Virginia, and Rhode Island. Twelve states sent delegates to the Constitutional Convention. Rhode Island was the only state to refuse to send delegates; critics said that this was because certain persons in charge of the government profited from the state's practice of issuing inflated paper money. This profit might end if the convention was successful in changing the Articles of Confederation.

Few of the convention delegates arrived in Philadelphia by the official May 14 starting date. James Madison arrived first, by stagecoach, on May 3. He brought boxes of books that he had borrowed from his friend Thomas Jefferson. Madison, who liked to be prepared, would study the books after convention meetings adjourned for the day.

George Washington was the second delegate to arrive in Philadelphia. He rode into town in his private carriage on May 13, greeted by cheering crowds and a military honor guard.

Those delegates from Pennsylvania who lived in Philadelphia, including Benjamin Franklin, Jared Ingersoll, and Robert Morris, did not have to travel far to the convention.

The remaining delegates were late for two reasons. Some were also members of the national Congress, which was in session in New York City at the same time that the Constitutional Convention was to begin. Also, travel—by horseback, stagecoach, private carriage, or boat—was slow in the best of weather. That year's heavy spring rains had muddied dirt roads and flooded streams, adding days to the already long travel times.

By May 25, delegates from seven states had arrived— enough for a quorum, the number of persons needed to conduct business legally. On that date, the Constitutional Convention was officially called to order. The delegates met in the Long Room of the Pennsylvania State House, the same room where the Declaration of Independence had been signed eleven years earlier.

The delegates decided not to release to the public any information about their meetings until the end of the convention. They were concerned that they could not debate freely if others were criticizing or otherwise trying to influence their decisions.

To preserve secrecy, all the windows and doors in the meeting hall were kept closed while the convention was in session. Inside the stuffy room, convention delegates suffered. The men from the northern states sweltered in their heavy woolen suits. Men from the southern states, who were accustomed to the heat, wore lighter clothing, but all the delegates suffered in the powdered wigs, long-sleeved shirts, long suit coats, silk stockings, and knee-length trousers worn by men at that time.

The Pennsylvania State House, now known as Independence Hall, still stands in Philadelphia, Pennsylvania.

The work of the convention delegates was to revise the Articles of Confederation, which had loosely governed the thirteen American states since 1781. Most states agreed that changes to the Articles were necessary, but opinions varied as to how many and what kind of changes should be made.

Some delegates, including George Washington, Benjamin Franklin, Alexander Hamilton, and James Madison, believed that the Articles of Confederation should be completely discarded. They wanted to create a new constitution that would provide for a strong national government.

Most of the states were against making too many changes to the Articles of Confederation. They were concerned that sweeping revisions to the Articles would create a powerful national government that would rob states of their rights. In fact, the states had made it clear to their delegates that they were not to bargain away states' rights. Credentials issued by Delaware to delegates George Read and John Dickinson actually forbade them to agree to any revision of the Articles that denied the small states equal voting rights in a national Congress.[1]

★ Delegate Diversity

A total of sixty-nine to seventy-four delegates were appointed to the convention. (Historical sources vary in their accounts of the number of delegates chosen.) Fifty-five delegates actually arrived in Philadelphia. Of those, twenty-nine attended every convention session. Most of those who missed sessions did so because of personal and family illness, private business, or service in the national Congress. A few delegates missed sessions because they were bored, or because they disapproved of the new national government under construction.

| George Washington, who was president of the convention, was one of the older convention delegates. | Eighty-one-year old Benjamin Franklin, from Philadelphia, was the oldest delegate to the convention | Jonathan Dayton, a New Jersey delegate, was the youngest delegate to the convention, at twenty-six. |

The convention delegates were lawyers, planters, merchants, and professional men. Forty-four of the fifty-five delegates had served or were presently serving in the national Congress. Twenty-one were veterans of the American Revolution against Great Britain. Eight had signed the Declaration of Independence. Six had signed the Articles of Confederation. Two delegates—Roger Sherman of Connecticut and Robert Morris of Pennsylvania—had signed both the Declaration of Independence and the Articles of Confederation, and would also sign the Constitution.

The average age of convention delegates was forty-two. Twenty-one delegates were under forty. Fourteen were fifty or over. George Washington, who was president of the convention, was fifty-five. Jonathan Dayton, a New Jersey delegate, was the youngest, at twenty-six. Eighty-one-year-old Benjamin Franklin, from Philadelphia, was the oldest.

Some of the nation's most influential statesmen did not attend the convention. For instance, John Adams and Thomas Jefferson were out of the country when the delegates met in Philadelphia. (John Adams later served as the nation's second President. Thomas Jefferson was elected the third President of the United States.) At the time of the convention, Jefferson was minister to France, and Adams was on duty as ambassador to the Court of St. James in London.

Patrick Henry, an outspoken patriot of the American Revolution, was also absent. He favored preserving the independence of the states, and did not want a strong national government. Though he was asked to be a delegate to the convention, Henry said he "smelt a rat," and refused to attend.[2]

★ Convention Business

For nearly four months, from May 25 through September 17, the delegates met six days a week, six hours a day. The convention recessed just two times. The delegates took one day off to celebrate the Fourth of July, and ten days in July and August to rest and conduct personal business. Through 400 hours of sessions, lasting 116 days, the delegates voted 566 times.

William Jackson was the elected secretary of Constitutional Convention, and he kept notes of the meetings. However, James Madison's convention notes were more complete, and they have most often been used by historians. Madison is also credited with writing the Virginia Proposal, which served as a blueprint for the Constitution. For his contributions, Madison has been called the Father of the Constitution.

The Constitution was signed in the Pennsylvania State House. This is an engraving by John Serz that shows the state house as it looked in 1776.

Forty-one delegates attended the final session of the convention on September 17, 1787. Of that group, thirty-nine signed the final draft of the Constitution. As president of the convention, George Washington was the first to sign. George Read of Delaware signed for himself and for his colleague, John Dickinson, who had become ill and left the convention a few days earlier.

Three delegates refused to sign the final draft of the Constitution. They were Elbridge Gerry of Massachusetts, and Edmund Randolph and Colonel George Mason, both of Virginia. Gerry opposed the formation of a strong central government. All three strongly believed the Constitution should have included a bill of rights.

Though it seemed many times that the convention would break up when tempers flared, compromises were made. Finally, despite the suffocating heat and heated arguments, the delegates hammered out the Constitution of the United States, creating a new national government.

★ A "Child of Fortune"

After the convention adjourned, George Washington wrote a letter to his close friend in Paris—the French nobleman and political leader Marquis de Lafayette. Lafayette had served as a general in the American army during the American Revolution, under Commander in Chief Washington. Washington was fond of Lafayette, and wrote to him often. In his letter to Lafayette, Washington said of the new Constitution:

> It is now a Child of fortune, to be fostered by some and buffeted by others. What will be the General opinion on, or the reception of it, is not for me to decide, nor

shall I say any thing for or against it: if it be good, I suppose it will work its way good; if bad, it will recoil on the Framers.[3]

George Washington could not know it then, but the founding fathers of the United States Constitution had created a remarkable piece of work. They had written a four-thousand-word document that remains to this day the world's oldest continuing written constitution.

2

Creating a Constitution

The first American colonists were mostly farmers, merchants, traders, and small manufacturers. They had come to America seeking a better way of life. Although they had learned to fear powerful (and often cruel) national governments, they soon realized that some form of organized, centralized rule was needed.

★ Freedom's English Roots

The model for defining liberty as written law was the Magna Carta. The Magna Carta (Latin for "Great Charter") was written in 1215. When England's King Richard, who was also known as Richard the Lion-Hearted, died in 1199, his brother John became king. King John soon fought with Pope Innocent III over who should be appointed archbishop of Canterbury. In England at that time, bishops were powerful leaders, and King John wanted to choose an archbishop who would not work against him. When the Pope defied the king and installed his own choice for archbishop of Canterbury, King John struck back by seizing church property.

The king of France sided with the Pope, and King John went to war with France. The conflict with the church ended when King John gave in and accepted the Pope's choice for archbishop. The king had financed the war with France by heavily taxing landowning barons,

The model for defining liberty as written law was the Magna Carta. Here, King John signs the Magna Carta giving the barons rights that they did not have before.

and the barons rebelled, demanding that King John sign a charter giving them certain rights. The king refused, and the barons renounced their loyalty to him. In order to save his throne, King John was forced again to back down. At a place called Runnymede, King John signed the Magna Carta.

The Magna Carta gave the barons personal freedoms that they had not had before. It read, in part:

> No free man shall be taken or imprisoned or deprived of his freehold or of his liberties or free customs, or outlawed, or exiled, or in any manner destroyed, nor shall we [the king] go upon him, nor shall we send upon him, except by a legal judgment of his peers or by the law of the land.[1]

Although the barons who were responsible for the signing of the Magna Carta acted only for themselves, the nobility, the document became a part of English law, and over time its freedoms were given to all English citizens.

★ Liberty in the New World

On colonial American soil, in 1620, the Pilgrims of the Massachusetts Bay Colony established a community government based on an agreement called the Mayflower Compact. They set up their own government, even though King James I of England had not given them the authority to govern themselves. The Mayflower Compact provided for framing "such just and equall lawes, ordinances, acts, constitutions, and offices," as the Pilgrims thought "most meete and convenient for the generall good of the Colonie."[2]

Ten years later, the Puritans who settled in Massachusetts used their corporate charter for a trading company as the basis for a civil government. The Massachusetts Bay Charter granted the power to make "Lawes and Ordinances for the Good and Welfare of the saide Companye, and for the Government and orderings of the saide Landes and Plantation, and the People inhabiting and to inhabite the same."[3]

Throughout the 1600s, as other groups of settlers arrived in America they, too, devised charters or compacts that set up local governments. Such charters included the Fundamental Orders of Connecticut (1639), and the Articles of Confederation of the United Colonies of New England (1643–1684).

★ A United States Government Takes Form

Early American colonists were subjects of the British Crown, and they were often dissatisfied with English law. For example, the colonists strongly objected to the Stamp Act of 1765, which taxed all newspapers and legal papers in the Colonies. After the law was passed, angry colonists took action by asking for delegates to attend a Stamp Act Congress in New York. Nine colonies sent delegates. At the Stamp Act Congress, delegates denounced what they called "taxation without representation."

In 1773, the British government again angered Americans by giving a British company the right to sell tea directly to the Colonies. This undercut the American merchants who had been selling British tea in the Colonies. In an act of defiance, colonists dressed as Native Americans boarded a British ship in a Boston harbor and dumped crates of tea overboard. The British government punished the colonists by briefly closing Boston ports. This only made the colonists more determined to fight the king's rule.

Shortly after the Boston Tea Party, Great Britain's Parliament passed a law levying a tax on tea. In response,

In an act of defiance against the British government, American colonists disguised as Native Americans boarded a British ship in Boston harbor and dumped crates of tea overboard.

colonists convened the First Continental Congress (also called the national Congress) in Philadelphia. To protest the British Tea Act of 1774, delegates from the thirteen colonies passed resolutions calling for a boycott, a ban against British trade.

After the first shots were fired in the American Revolution in 1775, delegates to the second national Congress gathered to form the Continental Army. George Washington was chosen commander in chief of the American army. However, Congress did not have the power to levy taxes to raise money for supplies to fight the war. The states were asked to give money to the army. Funds were scarce, so the army was poorly supplied.

When the national Congress met again in June 1776, a resolution was introduced that the "United Colonies are, and of right ought to be, free and independent States." A committee was appointed to "prepare a declaration to the effect of the said first resolution."[4] The result was the Declaration of Independence, which was adopted on July 4, 1776.

The American Revolution ended in 1781 with the defeat of the British by the American volunteer army. Independence brought new problems. The Articles of Confederation, passed by the national Congress that same year, showed the states' reluctance to give up power to a national government.

The Articles created one legislative body, called Congress. Each state had one vote in Congress. Only the states could regulate commerce, levy taxes, maintain an army, or print money. Consequently, Congress had no authority to levy taxes to pay off the $42 million debt from the American Revolution.

Under the Articles, the United States was simply a loose-knit group of bickering and competing states. Important legislation seldom passed, since it took agreement by nine states to pass laws.

★ Calling for a Constitutional Convention

After the American Revolution, several additional problems arose that called for establishing a stronger national government than was in effect under the Articles of Confederation:

- Spain was keeping settlers out of the east bank of the Mississippi River.

- Great Britain had ignored some of the provisions of the 1783 Treaty of Paris, which had formally recognized American independence after the American Revolution.

- Many state governments were ignoring citizens' rights. They seized private property in payment for bad debts, canceled contracts at will, threatened ships belonging to neighboring states, and imposed high taxes.

Squabbles among the states over trade led to a meeting at Annapolis, Maryland, in 1786. There were not enough delegates at the Annapolis Assembly for a quorum, and the meeting adjourned without any action being taken. Led by Alexander Hamilton and James Madison, the Annapolis Assembly delegates planned another meeting. They agreed to ask their state legislatures to send representatives to a meeting the following year in order to "devise such further provisions as shall appear to them necessary to render the constitution of the federal government adequate to the exigencies of the Union."[5]

The Liberty Bell, a symbol of the American revolution, is inscribed with the words, "Proclaim liberty throughout the land unto all the inhabitants thereof." The bell was rung to proclaim the signing of the Declaration of Independence.

An alarming event in January of 1787 made clear the need for a stronger national government. Eleven hundred farmers in Massachusetts, many of them veterans of the American Revolution, took up arms against the state government. The farmers hoped to force the state to issue paper money, so they could pay off their debts. They also tried to keep the courts from meeting to issue judgments for bad debts. Led by Daniel Shays, formerly a captain in the Continental Army, the group held off the state militia for five months before they were finally defeated. The weak national government could do nothing to help.

The possibility of armed revolt frightened the states. Seventeen days after Shays' Rebellion ended, they agreed to hold a convention to revise the Articles of Confederation, establishing a stronger federal government. The thirteen states could choose as many delegates as they wanted. (Though no number was assigned, most states could not afford to send a large number of delegates.) The delegates would assemble in Philadelphia, Pennsylvania, on the second Monday in May 1787.

★ The Convention Agenda

The delegates to the Constitutional Convention were instructed by their state legislatures to revise the Articles of Confederation to make them more effective in governing the states. They were not to sacrifice state sovereignty in the process; each state wanted to maintain its independence. However, each of the fifty-five delegates who traveled to Philadelphia had his own goals in mind. Some delegates believed a new Constitution should be written, creating a stronger national government. These delegates wanted to completely replace the Articles of Confederation.

After the first session of the convention was called to order on May 25, each delegate presented his credentials. Then, in order of occurrence:

- George Washington was elected president of the Convention.

- William Jackson was chosen secretary.

- The delegation agreed to keep all proceedings secret.

- Rules of procedure were established.

- A Committee of the Whole was formed. By calling their entire group the Committee of the Whole, the delegates could suspend rules of order and debate less formally.

★ The Virginia Proposal

The Virginia delegation had met together several times, in secret, before the convention began, so they arrived in Philadelphia ready to present their Virginia Proposal to the convention. On May 29, Virginia's Governor Edmund Randolph delivered a four-hour speech, urging the convention to adopt the Virginia Proposal. The plan, written primarily by James Madison, created a central republican form of government, in which the people would choose representatives to speak for them in government meetings. In a true democracy, a town meeting would have to be called for every governmental decision, so that all the people could debate and vote.

The resolutions of the Virginia Proposal laid the groundwork for the new government:

1. The government would consist of three branches: legislative, executive, and judicial.

George Washington (standing, center) presided over the Constitutional Convention of 1787.

2. A bicameral (two-house) legislature within the legislative branch would make laws.

3. Members of the first house of the legislature would be elected by a vote of the people, by a method yet to be determined.

4. Members of the second house of the legislature would be chosen by members of the first house.

5. The executive branch would enforce the law, and would be headed by a national executive, to be chosen by the legislature.

6. The judicial branch would interpret the law. A federal court—the national judiciary—would preside over the judicial branch.

7. Provision would be made for admitting new states to the Union.

8. Each state would be guaranteed a republican form of government.

9. The national Congress would be continued until a new government was established.

10. A method of amending the Constitution would be provided.

11. Officers of the states would be bound by oath to support the Union.

12. The Constitution would not become effective until it was ratified by special conventions of the people.

On May 30, the delegates voted in favor of the first resolution of the Virginia Proposal, "that a National Government ought to be established consisting of a supreme Legislative, Executive and Judiciary."[6]

★ The New Jersey Plan

As the delegation considered the complete Virginia Proposal, objections were raised. Some delegates feared that the proposed national government would hold too much power over the states. William Paterson's New Jersey Plan, introduced on June 15, addressed these fears. The New Jersey Plan provided for changes in the Articles of Confederation that would let Congress tax imports and regulate trade, but would preserve state power.

The New Jersey Plan was actually written by the delegates from New Jersey, New York, Delaware, Connecticut, and Maryland. It had been quickly prepared, and it was not as well thought out as the Virginia Proposal. Still, those delegates who felt they were being pushed too soon into creating a big, powerful government came to its defense. John Lansing of New York argued that the New Jersey Plan was more in line with the original intentions of the states, to revise the Articles of Confederation. Speaking of the Virginia Proposal, he said, "Is it probable that the states will adopt and ratify a scheme which they have never authorized us to propose?"[7]

The New Jersey Plan differed from the Virginia Proposal in several ways. In nine resolutions, it created:

- a single legislature, instead of a legislature made up of two branches or houses.

- a government that relied on the authority of state governments, rather than on the authority of the people.

- more than one executive, instead of one chief executive.

- one vote in the legislature for each state.

In short, the plan allowed each state to keep its independence. It did not prevent the states from violating foreign treaties, or from entering into treaties, or wars, individually. Nor did the plan keep a state from issuing paper money. James Madison argued that the New Jersey Plan would increase competition among the states over trade, settling western lands, fishing rights, and many other issues. Therefore, Madison insisted, Paterson's plan did not improve on any of the flaws of the Articles of Confederation.

The New Jersey Plan and the Virginia Proposal were sent back to the Committee of the Whole. In private, John Dickinson of Delaware scolded James Madison for pushing the Virginia Proposal so early in the convention:

> You see the consequence of pushing things too far. Some of the members from the small states wish for two branches in the general legislature and are friends to a good national government; but we would sooner submit to a foreign power than submit to be deprived of an equality of suffrage in both branches of the legislature and thereby be thrown under the domination of the large states.[8]

After several days of debate, on June 19 the delegation voted to reject the New Jersey Plan, and to consider seriously the Virginia Proposal. Many of the delegates were more afraid of anarchy—lawlessness—or of states becoming independent dictatorships than they were of a stronger national government Therefore, the Virginia Proposal was finally approved as the plan to be used in constructing the new government.

Approval of the Virginia Proposal meant that delegates were now committed to drafting a new Constitution, rather than simply patching up the old Articles of Confederation.

A Slave-Coffle passing the Capitol.

Slaves wearing handcuffs and shackles passing the United States Capitol in Washington, D. C., around 1815. According to the Great Compromise, a census would be taken regularly. This population count would be based on the number of free citizens, and on three-fifths of all slaves. (A slave was to be counted as three-fifths of one white person.)

★ Convention Clashes

After the delegation agreed to reexamine the Virginia Proposal, the next order of business for the Committee of the Whole was to debate and vote on each point of the proposal.

Delegates had quickly approved a two-house legislature. Now a bitter argument arose over the method of choosing legislators. Delegates from the smaller states did not want representation based on population or wealth. They argued that this would give the larger states a majority of the seats in the legislature. This meant the larger states would have an unfair voting advantage. Southern states insisted that slaves be counted as part of the general population, in any plan using population to determine representation. This was, of course, opposed by the northern states.

Questions also arose over choosing a national executive. Should the executive branch be headed by one man, or by a three-person group? Should the people or Congress choose the national executive? How long should the national executive serve, and should he (or they) be allowed to serve more than one term? Should he be given veto power? Should he be paid for his services? Would he be less likely to be corrupted if he served without pay?

As the convention moved into June, July, and then August, delegates' tempers often flared. Early in July, Alexander Hamilton went home angry; he and his two fellow delegates from New York had disagreed on every issue. Hamilton returned later, when George Washington asked him to come back. Robert Yates and John Lansing, the other two delegates from New York, left the convention and did not return. Yates and Lansing claimed the delegates had overstepped their charge in throwing out the Articles of Confederation. Maryland's delegates—Luther Martin and John Francis Mercer—also quit the convention. They opposed the Constitution's provisions for a strong central government.

As some delegates left, others arrived. New Hampshire had chosen two delegates—John Langdon and Nicholas Gilman—but the state's shortage of money had kept the two men at home. Finally Langdon, a wealthy businessperson, offered to pay expenses for himself and Gilman. The two New Hampshire delegates arrived at the convention on July 23.

★ The Great Compromise

As the hot summer days wore on, it was clear that without compromise the convention would become hopelessly deadlocked. To keep the convention from breaking up, delegates formed committees to forge compromises on key issues.

One key issue at the convention was fair representation in Congress. The problem was that large and small, wealthy and poor, and northern and southern states all had to be fairly represented. Several committees were appointed to find solutions, to decide how delegates would be chosen. In mid-July the following committee proposals were considered by the convention:

- Votes in the lower house of the legislature (later called the House of Representatives) would be based on direct taxation, which would be based on population. Therefore, larger states could elect more representatives than could the smaller states.

- A census would be taken regularly. This population count would be based on the number of free citizens, and on three-fifths of all slaves. (A slave was to be counted as three-fifths of one white person.)

- The number of members in the upper house (later called the Senate) would be the same for each state. This would give each state an equal vote.

On July 16, the delegates narrowly approved the proposals. This agreement concerning representation in Congress has since been named the Great Compromise.

The delegates of the Constitutional Convention of 1787 met in this Assembly Room, in Independence Hall. As the hot summer days wore on, tempers in this room would often flare.

★ The Committee of Detail

By the end of July, the convention delegates were exhausted from long days of debate. On July 26, they voted to adjourn for ten days to rest. However, so that the time would not be wasted, a five-man Committee of Detail was appointed to meet during the recess. John Rutledge of South Carolina chaired the committee. Other committee members included Oliver Ellsworth of Connecticut, Nathaniel Gorham of Massachusetts, Edmund Randolph of Virginia, and James Wilson of Pennsylvania.

The Committee of Detail dealt first with naming the parts of the new government. They proposed that the national legislature be called the Congress of the United States. The two houses of Congress would be called the House of Representatives and the Senate. The head of the executive branch of the government would be called the President of the United States.

The Committee of Detail suggested that the President serve with a Vice President. The Vice President would replace the President if for any reason the President could not serve. The Vice President would also preside over the Senate, voting only in case of a tie. The President and Vice President would be paid from the national treasury, and the President would have the power to veto legislation.

In just eight days, the Committee of Detail drafted a Constitution consisting of a preamble and twenty-three articles. On August 6, when the convention reconvened after the recess, the Committee of Detail presented its draft of the new Constitution. The 3,500-word document was read aloud by convention secretary William Jackson. The next order of business was for the entire delegation to review this document carefully.

James Madison was a member of the Committee on Postponed Matters. Later known as the Father of the Constitution, he was to become the fourth President of the United States.

★ Tying Up Loose Ends

By August 31, the delegates had considered all the recommendations of the Committee of Detail. A few loose ends remained. Among matters left to be resolved were election of the President, treaty-making, appointment power, trying impeachments, and money bills in Congress. A Committee on Postponed Matters (sometimes called the Committee of Unfinished Business) was appointed to consider these issues. New Jersey's David Brearley chaired the committee. Other committee members included Abraham Baldwin, Pierce Butler, John Dickinson, Nicholas Gilman, Rufus King, James Madison, Gouverneur Morris, Roger Sherman, and Hugh Williamson.

On September 4, the Committee on Postponed Matters presented its recommendations to the convention. The committee had devised a complex method of electing the President. The President would be elected by an electoral college. The members, called electors, would be chosen by the states. The President's term was set at four years, with no limits on reelection. The President would have the authority to make treaties. He would also appoint ambassadors, judges, and other officials, including Justices of the Supreme Court. The President's appointments would need the approval of the Senate.

The Committee on Postponed Matters suggested that the Senate try impeachment cases. They said that money bills should originate in the House of Representatives.

★ The Committee of Style

The measures introduced by the Committee on Postponed Matters were finally approved. On September 8, the last committee of the convention—the Committee of Style—was appointed to put the finishing touches on the Constitution. The five members of the Committee of Style included Alexander Hamilton, William Samuel Johnson, Rufus King, James Madison, and Gouverneur Morris. Johnson served as chairman of the committee.

Suggestions made by the Committee of Style were submitted to the entire convention on September 12. From September 13 to September 15 the delegates carefully reviewed each point. Final adjustments were made. Delegates agreed that the states should hold conventions to approve the way the Constitution had been written. A Bill of Rights was proposed, but a majority of the weary delegates voted to postpone debate on this issue until a later date, after the Constitution had been ratified.

The Committee of Style reduced the twenty-three articles to seven:

- The first article dealt with the legislative branch— Congress.

- The second discussed the executive branch—the President and Vice President.

- The third set up the judicial branch, including the Supreme Court.

- The fourth governed relations between the states.

- The fifth set down the method for amending the Constitution.

- The sixth declared the supremacy of federal law and of the Constitution.

- The seventh concerned ratification of the Constitution by the states.

Though few of the delegates were completely satisfied with the results of their labor, the United States Constitution was finally ready to be signed.

On Monday, September 17, the convention met for the last time to sign the Constitution. Benjamin Franklin urged fellow delegates to sign. He hoped that "every member of the Convention who may still have objections to it [the Constitution], would, with me, on this occasion doubt a little of his own infallibility, and . . . put his name to this instrument."[9]

★ After the Signing

In less than four months, the delegates to the Constitutional Convention had done the impossible. They carefully worked out a series of compromises that would govern the United States through the next two centuries and beyond.

After the delegates signed, six steps were needed to give legal force to the Constitution and to put into action the new national government:

1. The finished document would be presented to the national Congress in New York. Approval or disapproval was not necessary.

2. State ratifying conventions would be held. A "yes" vote by nine states would be needed for ratification.

3. Congress would determine the date for electors to be appointed by the states, and the date for electors to vote for the President and Vice President.

4. Elections of members of the House of Representatives and Senate would be held.

On September 17, 1787, the delegates met one last last time to sign the Constitution. This painting, *Signing of the Constitution* by Howard Chandler Christy, depicts that historic day.

5. The Congress of the United States would meet to count electoral votes for the President and Vice President.

6. The duly installed Congress and the President of the United States would begin their terms and would enact the Constitution.[10]

3

Resolving Major Issues

In February of 1788, just over four months after the Constitutional Convention adjourned, George Washington again wrote to his friend the Marquis de Lafayette:

> It appears to me, then, little short of a miracle, that the Delegates from so many different States (which States you know are also different from each other), in their manners, circumstances, and prejudices, should unite in forming system of national Government, so little liable to well founded objections.[1]

Clearly, drafting the Constitution was a huge task. The framers had worked hard to chisel out every article, line by line and word by word.

★ The Legislative Branch and Congress

Because the United States Congress would be central in initiating new legislation, the framers of the Constitution dealt first with the legislative branch of government.

On June 21, delegates to the Constitutional Convention voted to establish a bicameral Congress. The question of determining representation in Congress was resolved in mid-July, when the committee of eleven presented a solution that was approved by the convention. This was the Great Compromise discussed in chapter 2.

Article I of the Constitution, as it was finally written by the Committee of Detail, concerned the legislative branch of the government. It explained the composition, qualifications, rules, privileges, duties, and powers of Congress. It provided rules for impeachment of members of Congress. It also covered control of congressional elections, the procedure for passing bills, and the veto process. In addition, Article I limited certain powers of the states.

★ The Executive Branch and the President

Questions about the national executive were also difficult for convention delegates to resolve. Because the executive branch had not existed under the Articles of Confederation, there was no basis in the history of government for a chief executive such as the one the framers invented.

The Virginia Proposal said a national executive should be chosen by the legislative branch for a fixed term, but it did not go into detail. A few delegates even argued in favor of establishing a monarchy. Hugh Williamson of North Carolina warned that a single national executive could someday become an elected king:

> He will spare no pains to keep himself in for life, and will then lay a train for succession of his children. It [is] pretty certain . . . we should at some time or other have a King; but [I wish] no precaution to be omitted that might postpone the event as long as possible.[2]

Shortly after Paterson presented his New Jersey Plan, Alexander Hamilton surprised the convention delegates by speaking for six hours about his own plan. Why not have a monarch, Hamilton asked. "If this Executive Magistrate [that he proposed] would be a monarch for life," so what? Hamilton said that he "had no scruple in declaring,

BRANCHES OF THE FEDERAL GOVERNMENT

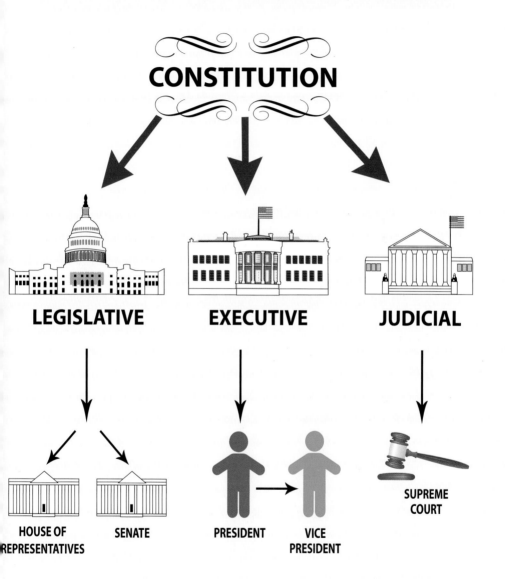

CONSTITUTION

LEGISLATIVE

EXECUTIVE

JUDICIAL

HOUSE OF REPRESENTATIVES

SENATE

PRESIDENT

VICE PRESIDENT

SUPREME COURT

supported as he was by the opinions of so many of the wise & good, that the British Government was the best in the world," and that he "doubted much whether any thing short of it would do in America."[3] There were few comments about Hamilton's plan, and it was not put to vote.

Convention delegates also disagreed over the President's salary. Some delegates believed that the President should serve without pay. Others believed that a President who served without pay would be corrupted and, in a way, owned by outside interests. (No one in 1787 could foresee today's expensive election campaigns, or the influence of the special interest groups that give money to political campaigns.)

A few delegates wanted state legislatures to pay the salaries of both the members of Congress and the President. Others pointed out that this could lead to special consideration for states' interests, over those of the national government.

Opinions also differed about the method for choosing the national executive. On one side were those who thought Congress was best qualified to choose. On the other side were those delegates who believed the people should have a voice in choosing their national executive.

Battle lines were drawn between large and small states. The smaller states wanted Congress to choose the national executive, because if the general population elected the President, states with fewer voters would have less say than the larger states with more voters. Large states were opposed to having Congress choose the chief executive. They knew they would have an advantage if their larger voting populations were allowed to choose the national executive. Some delegates believed a national executive chosen by Congress would be indebted to and too easily controlled by the members of Congress.

In early September, the Committee on Postponed Matters presented a plan for electing the President. The plan was complicated, but it met the requirements of every interest group among the delegates. Electors, making up the electoral college, would be chosen by their state legislatures. Each state would have as many electors as it had national Congressmen. The electors would meet and vote for two candidates. The candidate receiving a majority of votes would become President. The other candidate would become Vice President.

The electoral college method of electing the President was approved by a majority of states on September 6.

Article II of the Constitution, which covers the executive branch, provided that the national executive, called a President:

- would be elected by an electoral college.

- would serve a four-year term, without limit on reelection.

- would receive his salary from the national treasury.

- could make treaties, with approval of two-thirds of the Senate.

- could make appointments, subject to Senate confirmation.

The Committee of Detail proposed that the office of national executive be titled the President of the United States, and the holder of the office addressed as "His Excellency." The first three Presidents (George Washington, John Adams, and Thomas Jefferson), however, were uncomfortable with such a regal-sounding title, and it was seldom used. When James Madison became the nation's fourth president in 1809, he suggested that others call him "Mr. President." That practice has continued to the present day.

★ The Judicial Branch

Convention delegates argued less over the judicial branch than they did over the legislative and executive branches. The Virginia Proposal called for "one or more supreme tribunals"

The Supreme Court as it appeared in 2011. Standing left to right are Sonia Sotomayor, Stephen G. Breyer, Samuel Alito, Jr, and Elena Kagan. Seated left to right are Clarence Thomas, Antonin Scalia, Chief Justice John G. Roberts, Anthony M. Kennedy and Ruth Bader Ginsburg.

and "lesser tribunals," to be appointed by the national legislature. These "tribunals" would try cases involving crimes at sea, foreigners, citizens of different states, the collection of national taxes, impeachments, and other matters affecting the nation's peace and harmony.

There was little disagreement over establishing tribunals, but delegates did not agree over the method of appointing judges. Some thought the chief executive should appoint all judges. Others argued that this would give the President the power of a monarch, which the framers wanted to avoid at all costs. Other suggestions were that Congress appoint judges, or that the Senate alone make judicial appointments. The matter was postponed for final resolution until later in the convention. As the Constitution was finally written, the President was given the power to appoint Supreme Court Justices and some federal judges, with confirmation by the Senate.

The delegates also had to decide whether or not the national government should establish, in addition to the Supreme Court, lesser federal courts scattered throughout the states. These lesser federal courts would have final jurisdiction in some cases.

Again, delegates who stood strongly for states' rights opposed the establishment of federal courts other than the Supreme Court. However, delegates in favor of a strong central government argued that the judicial branch would

President Barack Obama delivering the annual State of the Union Address to Congress, January 25, 2011. This address is mandated in the Constitution.

be weakened without the help of lesser federal courts to hear certain cases. As a compromise, the convention agreed to let Congress decide whether or not to establish lower federal courts.

The convention proclaimed that judges could serve "during good behaviour," and that the Supreme Court would hear "all cases arising under the Constitution and the laws."[4] Article II, Section 4 stated that as "civil officers of the United States," federal judges could be removed from office "on impeachment for, and conviction of, treason, bribery, or other high crimes and misdemeanors."

The Supremacy Clause in Article VI of the Constitution said that all state and federal judges were to follow the Constitution, above all other laws, in deciding cases. This clause also prevented the states or Congress from passing laws contrary to the Constitution.

★ Other Important Provisions

The Two-thirds Vote. A major weakness of the Articles of Confederation was that a two-thirds vote of the states represented (a total of nine at that time) was needed to pass any measure. That meant that few important measures were passed. Therefore, in Article I, Section 5 of the Constitution, the framers said that a majority of each house would constitute a quorum to do business. However, on some important matters, the two-thirds vote was kept. A two-thirds vote would be required for:

- conviction by impeachment—vote of the Senate.

- treaties with foreign countries—approved by the Senate.

- expelling a member of Congress—vote by either house.

- passing a bill over the President's veto—vote by both houses.

- proposed constitutional amendments—vote by both houses, before submission to the states for ratification.

- election of the President, when no candidate received a vote of the majority of the electors—vote by the House of Representatives.

Slavery*. Many of the delegates attending the Constitutional Convention did not approve of slavery, though some who expressed disapproval were themselves slave owners. Slave owners who disapproved of slavery believed that keeping slaves was morally wrong, but they considered the practice a business necessity.

Sixteen of the convention delegates owned what they called "productive" slaves, those who were not "domestic," or household servants. These delegates were George Washington, all of the South Carolina delegation, Daniel of Saint Thomas Jenifer, George Mason, Edmund Randolph, John Blair, Richard Dobbs Spaight, and Alexander Martin. Domestic slaves were kept by James Madison, James Wilson, George Wythe, Robert Morris, John Dickinson, George Read, William Samuel Johnson, William Livingston, and Luther Martin.[5]

Though the final draft of the Constitution dealt with slavery in ten different provisions, the terms "slave" and "slavery" were not used. The Committee of Style used other words to refer to slaves, such as "other Persons," and "Person[s] held to Service or Labour."[6]

The southern states were allowed to count slaves according to the three-fifths ratio for determining representation in Congress. (The three-fifths ratio said that each slave would be counted as three-fifths of a person.)

The framers did not want to risk failure of the Constitution by forcing a judgment on the morality of slavery, so they agreed to give the slaveholding states several years to reconsider the custom. The further importation of slaves would be allowed to continue until the year 1808.

One delegate who opposed slavery in America—Gouverneur Morris—was particularly outspoken on the issue. He asked fellow delegates:

> Upon what principle is it that the slaves shall be computed in the representation? Are they men? Then make them Citizens and let them vote. Are they property? Why then is not other property included? The Houses in this City are worth more than all the wretched slaves which cover the rice swamps of South Carolina.[7]

The Constitution did not expressly forbid slavery until the Thirteenth Amendment was ratified in 1865.

Power of the States. The final version of the Constitution listed the powers given to Congress. All powers not listed in the Constitution remained with the states. States' requirements and restrictions were specifically listed in two sections of the Constitution. Restrictions were listed in Article I, Section 10, and requirements were listed in Article IV.

States were required to use gold or silver as legal tender, with all other mediums of exchange prohibited. This provision was made to establish a stable national economy. Before the American Revolution, there was no secure form of money in the Colonies. Land mortgages, furs, tobacco, and even Native American wampum were used as money, in exchange for goods and services. Later, under the Articles of Confederation, any state could print paper money at will. If the paper was not backed by something of value, such as gold, inflation resulted, and the paper money quickly became worthless. The Constitution stabilized the money situation, by transferring the power to issue money from the states to the federal government.

In 1791, during George Washington's first term as President, Congress passed a bill creating the Bank of the

United States. The bank was created to provide storage for government funds, and to issue bank notes that would provide a badly needed stable medium of exchange.

Before the Constitution was enacted, some state legislatures voided contracts, confiscated property, and reversed court judgments. State Governors had little power to prevent abuses. The Constitution prevented state governments from treading on the rights of citizens. Specifically, it prohibited the states from passing ex post facto laws, and laws voiding or hindering contracts. (An ex post facto law penalizes someone for an act performed in the past, before the new law against that act was passed.)

The Constitution also required states to respect the laws of other states, to hand over to each other fugitives from other states, and to grant equal privileges to citizens of other states. In short, states could no longer function as separate, independent countries.

Amendments to the Constitution. Article V set forth the process for amending the Constitution. Because they did not want it to be easy for future generations to change the Constitution, the framers invented a cumbersome process for amending it. Either the House of Representatives or the Senate can propose an amendment, but a two-thirds vote is required in both houses before an amendment can be sent to the states for ratification. Approval of three-fourths of the states, separately or in convention, is required before an amendment can be added to the Constitution.

One proposed amendment that did not survive the difficult amendment process was the Equal Rights Amendment (ERA). The ERA stated: "Equality of rights under the law shall not be denied or abridged by the United States or by any State on account of sex."[8] The ERA was passed by both houses of Congress and sent to the states in 1972.

Though the states were given seven years to ratify, then three more after that, they failed to do so. On June 30, 1982, when time ran out, the amendment was still three states short of the thirty-eight needed for ratification. A 1983 attempt to revive the ERA in Congress was unsuccessful.

Requirement of a Religious Test. Under Article VI of the Constitution, no religious oath may be required from a person holding an office in the federal government.

Article VI requires state and federal officeholders to take an oath to support the U.S. Constitution, but no mention is made of religion. (Article VI also provides that debts incurred by the government before the Constitution was adopted must be paid, and that the Constitution, federal laws, and treaties shall be the "supreme law of the land.")

Ratification of the Constitution. In Article VII, the delegates outlined the procedure for making the Constitution the law of the land. The document would first go to the Congress of the Confederation for review, although approval or disapproval of this group was not necessary before submission to the states. Copies would then be sent to the state legislatures, which were to hold ratification conventions. Ratification by nine states was necessary for the Constitution to be enacted.

There was no time limit for ratification but by June 1788, the required nine states had ratified the Constitution and it became effective.

★ The Push for Ratification

After the Constitution was delivered to them on September 20, 1787, the members of the Congress of the Confederation debated its good and bad points. According to critics, the document's two biggest faults were that it did not contain a bill of rights, and that it went beyond original intentions to revise the Articles of Confederation. Some

In October of 1787, James Wilson pointed out that it was not necessary to limit powers that Congress did not have anyway. Congress would have no powers not given to it by the Constitution, he said. Why worry about the government curbing religious freedom, for example, when the Constitution grants no such power of Congress over religion?

Edmund Randolph of Virginia argued that a bill of rights was not needed, because the purpose of a bill of rights was to limit the power of the king, and America no longer had a king.[3]

Those on the other side of the argument warned that certain rights must be listed in the Constitution as untouchable. Otherwise, they said, the government could not be trusted to respect those rights. George Mason, who had refused to sign the Constitution, became highly critical of the document toward the end of the convention. Mason published his "Objections to the constitution of Government Formed by the Convention" in various newspapers during November 1787. He wrote:

> There is no Declaration of Rights; and the Laws of the general Government being paramount to the Laws and Constitutions of the several States, the Declaration of Rights in the separate States are no Security. . . . This Government will commence in a moderate Aristocracy; it is at present impossible to foresee whether it will, in its Operation, produce a Monarchy, or a corrupt oppressive Aristocracy; it will most probably vibrate some Years between the two, and then terminate in the one or the other.[4]

From his post in Paris, Thomas Jefferson wrote to James Madison in December 1787 that a bill of rights was needed to protect a number of rights, including freedom of the press and religion. "A bill of rights is what the people are entitled to against every government on earth, general or particular, and what no just government should refuse, or rest on inference."[5]

The Federalists fought hard for ratification of the Constitution, and eventually they won the battle, but the public would not be swayed on the question of a bill of rights. "We must have a bill of rights" became the rallying cry for ratifying conventions held in each state in 1787 and 1788. The Constitution was finally approved, but with the condition that a list of individual liberties, expressly guaranteed by the new government, would be added immediately in the form of the Bill of Rights.

★ A Promise Kept

One of the first acts of the first Congress of the United States when it met in 1789 was to create the Bill of Rights. James Madison was among convention delegates who had voted against including a bill of rights, and he had argued on the Federalist side for ratification. However, politics changed Madison's mind. He had lost his first bid for a seat in the U.S. Senate, largely because he had opposed including a bill of rights in the Constitution. By the time he campaigned for a seat in the U.S. House of Representatives in 1788, Madison had been persuaded by Thomas Jefferson that a bill of rights would provide a necessary "legal check" to the powers of government.

U.S. Representative James Madison drafted a list of nineteen rights, compiled from more than two hundred suggestions received from the states. On June 8, 1789, Madison's list was submitted to the House of Representatives. A House committee reduced it to seventeen rights. The list was then sent on to the Senate. By September 25, 1789, both houses of Congress had agreed on twelve provisions. Finally, the new Bill of Rights was sent to each of the thirteen states for ratification.

By September 1789, both houses of Congress had agreed on a Bill of Rights with twelve provisions. Shown here is the original Bill of Rights, on display today in Washington, D.C.

New Jersey was the first state to ratify the Bill of Rights, on November 20, 1789. Eight more states soon followed. Because Vermont was admitted to the Union on March 4, 1791, eleven states had to ratify, in order to provide the necessary three–fourths vote required for adoption.

Virginia was the eleventh state to ratify, on December 15, 1791, and on that date the Bill of Rights became law. Accidentally, three states—Massachusetts, Connecticut, and Georgia—did not ratify the first ten amendments until the sesquicentennial celebration of the Constitution in 1939.[6]

Ten rights from the proposed list of twelve were accepted by the states for final ratification. Two of the twelve proposals submitted were rejected: One proposal called for enlarging the House of Representatives. The second prevented members of the House from raising their own pay.

★ States and the Bill of Rights

James Madison wanted to add an amendment that would make the Bill of Rights binding on state governments, as well as the federal government. Congress did not act upon Madison's suggestion. Later, this proved to be a mistake, as state laws were passed that trespassed on individual liberties.

The Fourteenth Amendment, ratified in 1868, made the Bill of Rights binding on state governments. The amendment states: "No State shall make or enforce any law which shall abridge the privileges or immunities of citizens of the United States."

This seemed to be a final victory for individual freedom, but throughout American history the Bill of Rights has been tested by laws that violate personal rights. The basic rights listed in the first ten amendments to the Constitution have had to be won repeatedly in the courts.

5

It's a Free Country

The United States Constitution and the Bill of Rights marked a first in the history of world governments. For the first time, written law preserving liberty was in place before a government assumed power. Surely, the framers reasoned, this would ensure that the government could not now violate the rights of the people.

However, history has shown that freedoms must be won over and over again. In the United States, when laws are passed that violate Constitutional rights, the court system can be asked to intervene. Lawsuits may be brought in defense of these rights. The legal decisions that result can declare challenged laws unconstitutional, or they can allow them to stand. Either way, court decisions set a legal precedent, a pattern for dealing with future problems.

★ The Rights to Pray, Speak, and Write

The First Amendment to the Constitution prohibits the government from limiting certain important freedoms of individual expression. It allows people to worship freely, to speak and write freely, to meet together peaceably, and to complain to and about the government. (See Appendix C, "The Bill of Rights.")

The First Amendment prevents the government from arresting anyone who criticizes the government in speech or in print. Before the American Revolution, a catch–all charge called seditious libel was used by the British government to punish colonists who dared to speak out against the government. Like many other rules imposed by the Crown, colonists considered seditious libel laws unjust.

Finally, without taking up arms, the colonists rebelled. In a 1734 landmark court case, a jury made up of American colonists ignored British law. They found the accused, John Peter Zenger, not guilty of four counts of seditious libel. Zenger, a printer in New York, was arrested for printing material critical of the territorial governor, who had been appointed by the king. British laws against seditious libel said that the government had only to prove that Zenger printed the material. Zenger admitted that he had. According to British law, Zenger was clearly guilty as charged. In court, the colonial jury ignored the law, and found Zenger not guilty. Zenger was the last colonist to be charged with seditious libel. This case established a basis for freedom of the press in America, before the American Revolution, and before the Declaration of Independence, the Constitution, and the Bill of Rights were written.[1]

The First Amendment also keeps "church and state" (religion and government) separate. Many settlers who came to America had suffered under foreign governments that forced them either to follow a particular religion or to pay a fine. The First Amendment was written to prevent the government from establishing a state religion that all citizens must support. It also prohibits the government from using public tax dollars to favor one religion over another.

★ Upholding the First Amendment

Recent court cases illustrate America's continuing efforts to preserve and to define the First Amendment. For instance, in 1993, a federal appeals court in New York upheld a lower

Separation of church and state continues to provoke debate.

court ruling that declared begging to be a form of free speech. The ruling was made after New York City's ban on panhandling on public streets and in public parks was challenged in court as unconstitutional.[2]

Other questions of free speech and the press that have been raised in the courts in recent years include:

- Does freedom of the press include school newspapers?

- Does freedom of speech and the press extend to computer users and networks?

- Can public officials claim damages for libel or slander for statements about their official conduct?

- Should the right to protest government policy include burning the American flag?

In 1989, in *United States v. Eichman,* the Supreme Court upheld the legal right of protestors to burn the flag. Justice William Brennan wrote his opinion of the ruling:

> If there is a bedrock principle underlying the First Amendment it is that the Government may not prohibit the expression of an idea simply because society finds the idea itself offensive or disagreeable. Punishing desecration of the flag dilutes the very freedom that makes the emblem so revered and worth revering.[3]

Religious freedom was upheld by a 1993 Supreme Court decision that struck down a Florida law banning the religious sacrifice of animals. The Court held that the law violated the rights of persons who practiced Santeria to observe their religion.

Separation of church and state is a First Amendment issue that frequently appears in court: Prayer in public schools is one example. In 1962, the U.S. Supreme Court declared organized prayer in public schools unconstitutional. Since then, the court has viewed most forms of officially

The First Amendment gives Americans the freedom to say, believe, and express almost anything we choose—no matter how offensive to others.

approved prayer in public schools as illegal under the First Amendment. This includes teacher–led prayer, moments of silence set aside for prayer, or even prayer by outside clergy at a graduation ceremony.

However, some forms of school prayer have been allowed. In 1992, in *Lee v. Weisman,* the Supreme Court ruled that clergy–provided prayer at public school graduation ceremonies was unconstitutional. That same year, in *Jones v. Clear Creek Independent School District* (Texas), the Fifth Circuit Court of Appeals ruled that "student–initiated" graduation prayer was legal. The Court said the graduation prayers in this case were not "government–sponsored" religious activity, because the students initiated them. This, the court said, was free speech, protected by the First Amendment.

The Supreme Court refused to review *Jones v. Clear Creek.* As a result, the decision became law in the three states that make up the Fifth Circuit: Texas, Louisiana, and Mississippi.[4]

Since the *Jones* case, federal district courts in Idaho and Florida have upheld school policies allowing student–initiated prayers at graduation. In addition, six states—Alabama, Georgia, Maryland, Mississippi, Tennessee, and Virginia—now permit a moment of silence during the day in public schools. Four others—Florida, Oklahoma, Pennsylvania, and South Carolina—have considered similar laws.[5]

In 1993, in *Kiryas Joel v. Grumet,* the Supreme Court struck down as unconstitutional a public school district created to serve the handicapped children of a small sect of Hasidic Jews. Due to village lines drawn in 1977, in Kiryas Joel, New York, the Kiryas Joel School District included only members of the Satmar Hasidim Jewish sect. Under federal law, handicapped children are entitled to publicly funded special education classes, and such classes in the Kiryas Joel District were taught in the Satmar private schools by public school teachers. Federal laws changed in the mid–1980s, and the Satmar handicapped children were expected to enroll in public schools. The sect objected, and the state legislature allowed members to create their own public school district. The court ruled that this violated the First Amendment's prohibition against the establishment of religion. However, in the decision, the Supreme Court then explained how the children could be lawfully helped.[6]

Separation of church and state continues to provoke debate. In the 1990s, those who strongly favored allowing prayer in public schools called for a constitutional amendment. A school prayer amendment, however, would conflict with Supreme Court opinions regarding the First Amendment and its ban against laws "respecting an establishment of religion." An amendment allowing prayer in public schools would require an amendment of the Bill of Rights—which has never been done.

★ Voting and Other Civil Rights

We assume that suffrage, the right to vote, is granted by the Constitution. The original document, however, makes few references to voting. Article I says that Americans who are eligible to vote for the largest house of their state legislature can vote for U.S. Representatives. The Seventeenth Amendment grants the same right concerning U.S. Senators.

In addition, Amendments Fifteen, Nineteen, Twenty–four, and Twenty–six ban discrimination against voters because of race, gender, failure to pay a tax, or age for those eighteen and over. Nothing is said about a general right to vote. The Fourteenth Amendment has been interpreted by the courts as covering voting rights, because it forbids a state to deny any person "the equal protection of the laws."

A woman auto mechanic at work. Under civil rights laws, employers, including the U.S. government, may not discriminate in hiring on the basis of race, religion, or gender.

The Thirteenth Amendment, ratified after the Civil War, abolished slavery in the United States. The Fourteenth and Fifteenth Amendments gave the full rights of citizenship to all Americans, regardless of "race, color, or previous condition of servitude."

However, for several decades the Southern states used Jim Crow laws to keep African–American citizens from voting and from exercising other personal liberties. The laws were named for a minstrel song that depicted African Americans as poor and simple. Literacy tests and grandfather clauses that said a person could not vote if descended from a slave kept many African Americans from voting. (Grandfather clauses based a new law on conditions that existed in the past.) Despite the Fourteenth and Fifteenth Amendments, segregation, the separation of the races, was the rule in the South for many years.[7]

The Supreme Court was not much help during this time. For instance, in a narrow interpretation of the Fourteenth Amendment in 1873, the Court held that the amendment applied only to "national rights," which included the right to travel or to petition the federal government. This ruling took away much of the force of the Fourteenth Amendment.

In *Plessy v. Ferguson,* the Supreme Court in 1896 held that if states offered "separate but equal" services for African Americans and whites, segregation was legal. This decision diluted both the Thirteenth and Fourteenth Amendments.[8]

The Civil Rights Act, passed in 1964, helped African Americans reclaim lost constitutional rights. The law has been upheld in many Supreme Court decisions.

The civil rights battle continues. For instance, some states recently formed new political districts that group voters of one race within certain boundary lines. Some districts were populated by persons of only one race. These voters might be predicted to vote a certain way in an election. In 1995, the Supreme Court declared these districts unconstitutional, as they limited voting along racial lines.

★ Rights Against Searches and Seizures

The Fourth Amendment protects U.S. citizens against unreasonable searches and seizures. This includes one's person, house, papers, and effects. Under this amendment, the police must have a warrant before they can perform certain searches, or arrest suspects for certain crimes.

Roadblock programs, in which the police stop all cars to test drivers' sobriety, have been challenged in court as a violation of the Fourth Amendment. In 1990, the Supreme

Roadblock programs, in which police stop all cars to test drivers' sobriety, have been challenged in court as a violation of the Fourth Amendment.

The Civil Rights Act, passed in 1964, helped African Americans reclaim lost constitutional rights. Leaders such as Martin Luther King, Jr., shown here speaking at the 1963 March on Washington, helped bring about these changes.

Court ruled that the practice in Michigan was not unconstitutional, since every car was being stopped, and no one was being singled out.[9]

In 1994, police searches for firearms in a Chicago housing project were challenged by the American Civil Liberties Union (ACLU), as a violation of Fourth Amendment rights of the residents involved. A federal judge ruled the searches unconstitutional. Though some residents who feared for the safety of their families wanted the searches to continue, others believed that it was more important to uphold civil liberties.[10]

Similarly, in a 1994 decision resolving *University of Colorado v. Derdeyn,* the U.S. Supreme Court upheld a ruling of the Colorado Supreme Court about drug testing in college sports. The Colorado Supreme Court had ruled that forcing college athletes to undergo random urine tests violates the Fourth Amendment. The school's drug screening program was called an unreasonable search and seizure.[11]

★ Rights of the Accused

The Fifth, Sixth, Seventh, and Eighth Amendments cover due process of law, which calls for fair methods in arrests and prosecutions.

Under the Fifth Amendment, civilians, persons not members of the military, who are accused of serious crimes in the United States have the right to a grand jury indictment. (Rules of military law are different than those for civilian law.) This means that a special jury must be called to decide whether or not the state has enough evidence to charge and bring an accused person to trial. If indicted by the grand jury, the accused must stand trial.

The Fifth Amendment also says that a person may not be tried more than once for the same offense; this is called double jeopardy. The double jeopardy clause works like this: An accused person is found not guilty of a crime. That defendant may not be tried again for the same crime. However, if a defendant is found guilty of a crime, and appeals the conviction, the conviction may be reversed because of an error made by the court at the first trial. Under most circumstances, the state may then try the defendant again for the same crime.[12]

A person may also be tried under state statutes, then again under federal laws. For example, on March 3, 1991, Los Angeles police officers stopped motorist Rodney King after a high–speed chase. King was pulled over and stepped out of his car. Later, the officers claimed that he resisted arrest, testifying that he was also intoxicated. In the scuffle that followed, officers beat King with their nightsticks. An observer videotaped the beating, and four police officers were charged by the state with assault. A jury found the four officers not guilty. This decision, in April of 1992, led to riots in which fifty–three persons were killed and a thousand were injured.

Later, the federal government brought charges against the four police officers for violating Rodney King's civil rights. In a second trial, in April of 1993, two of the four police officers were acquitted. Each of the two officers who were found guilty was sentenced to two and a half years in prison.

Rodney King sued the city of Los Angeles. In April 1994, a U.S. District Court jury awarded King $3.8 million for medical expenses, pain and suffering, and loss of future income.[13]

Under the Fifth Amendment, individuals may not be forced to testify against themselves. The amendment also prohibits the government from taking private property

Place _____

Date _____

Time _____

YOUR RIGHTS

1. You have the right to remain silent.

2. Anything you say can and may be used against you in a court of law.

3. You have the right to talk to a lawyer and have him present with you while you are being questioned.

4. If you cannot afford to hire a lawyer, if you wish one, a lawyer will be appointed to represent you before any questioning.

5. If you decide to answer questions now with or without a lawyer, you still have the right to stop the questioning at any time for the purpose of consulting a lawyer.

6. However, you may waive the right to advice of counsel and your right to remain silent, and you may answer questions or make a statement without consulting a lawyer if you so desire.

WAIVER

1. Do you understand each of these rights I have explained to you?

   _____

2. Having these rights in mind, do you wish to talk to us now?

   _____

Signed _____

Witness _____
Witness _____
Time _____

In 1966, the Supreme Court ruled that all suspects must be read their constitutional rights by arresting police officers. Shown here is a copy of those "Miranda" rights.

without "just compensation"—paying a fair price. In addition, the Fifth Amendment states that no person may be "deprived of life, liberty, or property, without due process of law."

The Sixth Amendment states that a person who is accused of a crime has the right to a speedy and public trial, by an impartial jury chosen in the state and district where the crime was committed. (Today's clogged court calendars often make "speedy" an unrealistic idea.) The amendment also says that accused persons must be informed of the "nature and cause" of the charges against them. Accused parties have the right to confront witnesses against them, and to find witnesses in their favor. They also have the right to hire an attorney in their defense.

Miranda v. Arizona, a case heard by the Supreme Court in 1966, fortified the rights of the accused under the Sixth Amendment. The Court found that police station questioning methods put too much pressure on the accused. The Court also held that accused persons did not always know their constitutional rights. The *Miranda* decision required the police to inform suspects of their rights at the beginning of the arrest process. Police must now tell suspects that they have the right to remain silent, that anything they say can and will be used against them in a court, and that they have the right to an attorney, even if they can't afford to hire one. In that case, the state will pay the legal fees.[14]

The Seventh Amendment guaranteed the right to a jury trial in certain civil suits.

The Eighth Amendment prohibited excessive bail, fines, and punishments for persons accused of a crime. The well-known term "cruel and unusual punishment" comes from this amendment. It means that persons accused of or jailed for a crime cannot be tortured, or otherwise subjected to extremely harsh punishment.

★ The Right to Privacy

The Constitution does not grant a specific right to privacy. However, it hints at this right by keeping the government out of private affairs. Also, the broad Ninth Amendment says that just because a right is not listed in the Constitution, that does not mean that it does not exist. In the words of the amendment, "The enumeration in the Constitution, of certain rights, shall not be construed to deny or disparage others retained by the people."

Several landmark Supreme Court decisions have preserved a person's right to privacy. For instance, in the much debated 1973 *Roe v. Wade* decision, the Supreme Court ruled that privacy includes a woman's decision to have an abortion during the first three months of a pregnancy.[15] Debate on both sides of the abortion issue continues. *Roe v. Wade* may yet be reversed, as new Justices are appointed to the Supreme Court, and as opinions are changed by new arguments.

Privacy concerns are often associated with sexual behavior. As long as laws are passed restricting or regulating such acts, these issues will continue to be in the news.

★ The Constitution and the Bill of Rights Endure

For more than two centuries, Americans have preserved the government created by the United States Constitution. According to historians, the Constitution and the government it created—a republic based on the principle of democracy—have lasted this long for two reasons: First, the Constitution created a political system that could be adapted to fit future needs. Second, the Constitution was written to control government, not people.

Is the death penalty cruel and unusual punishment?

Many questions remain about the rights of all Americans. Is the death penalty cruel and unusual punishment? Should women have an unconditional right to abortion? Is an Equal Rights Amendment necessary to give all individuals equal opportunity under the law?

Such issues will not be resolved soon, or without further debate and compromise. The promise of the American system of government is not that people will no longer disagree; it is that citizens have certain freedoms guaranteed to them. Most important, and rare among world governments, that promise is upheld, in writing, in the United States Constitution.

Appendix A: The Signers

Each of the thirty–nine delegates who signed the United States Constitution had his own hopes and goals for the future of the nation. The distinguished and influential Americans who signed the final draft of the Constitution are listed below, by state:

★ Connecticut

William Samuel Johnson, 50, a lawyer, backed the Great Compromise at the convention, and was appointed chairman of the Committee of Style. He worked for ratification in Connecticut, and later was a U.S. senator (1789–1791). He died on November 14, 1819.

Roger Sherman, 56, was a self–educated lawyer, cobbler, and almanac maker who played a leading role at the convention. He backed the Great Compromise and sat on the Committee of Postponed Matters. Sherman and Robert Morris of Pennsylvania were the only two convention delegates to sign all three of the nation's landmark documents: The Declaration of Independence, the Articles of Confederation, and the Constitution. Sherman was a U.S. congressman (1789–1791) and a U.S. senator (1791–1793). He died on July 23, 1793.

★ Delaware

Richard Bassett, 42, was a lawyer who also had been a soldier, a judge, a legislator, and a state governor. He was captain of a cavalry troop in the American Revolution. He attended most convention sessions, but served on no committees and was largely silent during debates. He was a U.S. senator (1789–1793). Bassett died on September 15, 1815.

Gunning Bedford, Jr., 40, was a lawyer. He graduated from the College of New Jersey, which is now Princeton University. He had been attorney general of Delaware, and had served as a member of the national Congress. He spoke often in convention debates, supporting small states' rights. He was a member of the Delaware Convention that ratified the Constitution. Bedford was appointed a U.S. district judge by President Washington in 1789. He died on March 30, 1812.

Jacob Broom, 35, a wealthy businessperson, diligently attended convention sessions, yet was one of the less well known signers of the Constitution. He served as the nation's first postmaster general (1790–1792). He died on April 25, 1810.

John Dickinson, 55, a lawyer, was a brilliant and respected convention delegate. He was known for *The Letters From a Farmer in Pennsylvania,* which he had written earlier, questioning the right of Britain's Parliament to tax the American colonies. He had been chairman of the congressional committee that wrote the Articles of Confederation, and he had served as governor of Delaware and of Pennsylvania. At the convention, Dickinson served as a member of the Committee on Postponed Matters. He became ill toward the end of the convention, and could not stay to sign, so he authorized George Read to sign for him. Dickinson died on February 14, 1808.

George Read, 54, a lawyer, signed the Declaration of Independence, and he was a delegate to the Annapolis Assembly in 1786. He was head of his state's delegation to the Constitutional Convention. At the convention he backed small states' rights and favored a strong chief executive. Under his leadership, Delaware was the first state to ratify the Constitution on December 7, 1789. Read served as a U.S. senator (1789–1793). He died on September 21, 1798.

★ Georgia

Abraham Baldwin, 33, had been a minister, lawyer, and educator. He was a chaplain in the Continental Army. After the war, he was a member of the Georgia state legislature and of the national Congress. At the convention, he was a member of the Committee on Postponed Matters. Though he represented Georgia at the convention, Baldwin voted with the smaller states for equal state representation in the Senate. His vote caused a tie that temporarily deadlocked the debate. Other delegates guessed that Baldwin caused the tie for one of two reasons: either he feared that the small states would leave the convention if they lost the vote, or, as a native of Connecticut (he had lived in Georgia just three years), he was influenced by Connecticut's Ellsworth, Sherman, and Johnson. Baldwin was a U.S. congressman (1789–1799) and he was a U.S. senator (1799–1807). He died on March 4, 1807.

William Few, 39, a lawyer, statesman, jurist, and banker, had one year of formal education. He, too, had served in the Georgia legislature and was a member of the national Congress when he was called to the convention. In fact, Few missed all of the July sessions, and part of those held in August, due to service in Congress. He did not participate in convention debates, but he did attend Georgia's ratifying convention, where he urged approval of the Constitution. Few later served as a U.S. senator (1789–1793), and he was a member of the New York General Assembly (1802–1805). After government service, Few was the director of Manhattan Bank (1804–1814) and he was president of the City Bank of New York. He died on July 16, 1828.

★ Maryland

Daniel Carroll, 57, who signed the Articles of Confederation in 1781, had been a member of the national Congress. At the convention, he supported election of the President by electors chosen by state citizens. As a delegate, he opposed payment of U.S. senators by their home states. He served as a Senator in the first U.S. Congress (1789–1793). Carroll died on May 7, 1796.

Daniel of Saint Thomas Jenifer, 64, was a planter and statesman. He served in the Maryland Senate (1777–1780) and in the national Congress (1779–1782). He was a close friend of George Washington. Although he did not take a leading part in the convention, Jenifer stayed to the end and signed the Constitution. He died on November 16, 1790.

James McHenry, 34, was a physician who had been educated in Dublin, Ireland. He served twice as a member of the Maryland Senate (1781–1786 and 1791–1796), and was a member of the national Congress (1783–1786). He missed many of the convention sessions, due to his brother's illness. McHenry kept a journal of the proceedings that later proved a valuable resource for historians. He signed the finished Constitution, and later served as U.S. Secretary of War (1796–1800). He died on May 3, 1816.

★ Massachusetts

Nathaniel Gorham, 49, a wealthy merchant who left school at the age of fifteen, was an excellent debater at the convention. He had been a state legislator (1781–1787), a judge of the Middlesex Court of Common Pleas (1785), and president of the national Congress (1786). He attended every session of the convention, serving as chairman of the Committee of the Whole, and as a member of the Committee of Detail. He died on June 11, 1796.

Rufus King, 32, a Harvard–educated lawyer, had served in the national Congress (1784–1786). Though one of the youngest convention delegates, he was also one of the most effective speakers. He attended every session. King supported the Virginia Proposal for a strong national government, and spoke against the further importation of slaves. He served on the Committee on Postponed Matters and the Committee of Style. King was a candidate for President of the United States in 1816, and twice ran for Vice President (1804 and 1808). He died on April 29, 1827.

★ New Hampshire

Nicholas Gilman, 32, a lawyer, had served two terms in the national Congress. During the convention he was a member of the Committee on Postponed Matters. The nation's third President, Thomas Jefferson, appointed him Commissioner in Bankruptcy in 1802. He was a member of the U.S. Senate (1805–1814). Gilman died on May 2, 1814.

   John Langdon, 46, was a wealthy merchant with broad political experience. He was a Revolutionary militia leader, member of the New Hampshire Legislature (1777–1781 and 1801–1805), and twice president [governor] of New Hampshire (1785–1786 and 1788–1789). When the state of New Hampshire could not pay travel expenses for delegates to the Constitutional Convention, Langdon paid them himself, rather than have the state go unrepresented. He was in favor of giving a national government strong powers of defense, taxation, and commerce, and he urged New Hampshire to ratify the Constitution. He was the first presiding officer of the U.S. Senate (1789), and governor of New Hampshire twice again (1805–1808 and 1810–1812). He died on September 18, 1819.

★ New Jersey

David Brearley, 42, had been a Revolutionary patriot and a judge on the New Jersey Supreme Court. He attended convention sessions regularly, and served as chairman of the Committee on Postponed Matters. He died on August 16, 1790.

   Jonathan Dayton, 26, a lawyer and graduate of Princeton University, was the youngest delegate to the convention. He arrived late, on June 21, but faithfully participated in convention debates. He supported payment of U.S. senators by the national treasury. Dayton signed the Constitution in spite of his doubts. He was a member of the first U.S. Congress under the Constitution, and served two additional terms. He died on October 9, 1824.

William Livingston, 64, a Yale graduate and a lawyer, was governor of New Jersey at the time of the convention. Others called Livingston the Whipping Post, because he was tall and thin. He seldom participated in debates, but he campaigned actively in his state for ratification of the Constitution. Livingston died on July 25, 1790.

William Paterson, 42, was a lawyer who had served as state attorney general. He earned a master's degree from the College of New Jersey in 1766, delivering an address on "Patriotism." Though he was born in Ireland, he fought for the patriots during the American Revolution. At the convention, he was chief spokesperson for the New Jersey Plan, calling for revision of the Articles of Confederation, rather than the drafting of a new Constitution. Paterson later became an Associate Justice to the United States Supreme Court (1793–1806), and he died on September 9, 1806.

★ New York

Alexander Hamilton, 30, was a lawyer, a graduate of Columbia University, and a nationalist. An intellectual and an excellent speaker, he was constantly outvoted by his two fellow delegates. He left the convention in disgust near the end of the first month but returned toward the end of the convention at George Washington's request. With James Madison and John Jay, he wrote *The Federalist Papers* explaining the Constitution and urging its ratification. Hamilton served as the first U.S. secretary of the Treasury under President George Washington. In 1804, his life ended tragically when he was killed in a duel with Aaron Burr.

★ North Carolina

William Blount, 38, merchant and western land speculator, served in the North Carolina state legislature and in the national Congress. After he left the convention on June 20 to attend the

North Carolina Assembly, he went on to New York to attend the national Congress. He returned to the convention August 3, and remained to sign the Constitution. Blount became governor of the Tennessee Territory in 1790, and was elected to the U.S. Senate when the territory became a state in 1796. In 1797, he became the first senator to be expelled from the U.S. Senate. Blount had lost money in land speculation, and he became involved in a scheme to transfer control of Spanish Florida and Louisiana to Great Britain. He was expelled from the Senate when his involvement was discovered. He died on March 21, 1800.

Richard Dobbs Spaight, 29, was educated at the University of Glasgow, in Scotland. He was not a leader at the convention but attended every session and spoke occasionally. He was a three–term governor of North Carolina, and a U.S. congressman (1798–1801). On September 6, 1802, at the age of forty–four, Spaight was killed in a duel with a political rival.

Hugh Williamson, 52, was a merchant and physician who had studied in Europe. Influential in convention debates, he served on five committees, including the Committee on Postponed Matters. He was a U.S. congressman (1789–1793), and he wrote many scientific studies. He died on May 22, 1819.

★ Pennsylvania

George Clymer, 48, lawyer, merchant, and banker, signed the Declaration of Independence, and served as a member of the national Congress (1776–1777) and of his state legislature (1785–1788). He attended convention sessions, but seldom spoke. He later served as a U.S. congressman, and he was the first president of The Bank of Philadelphia. He died on January 24, 1813.

Thomas FitzSimons, 46, a merchant, was born in Ireland, and came to America in 1760. He was a military officer in the American Revolution, and served in the Pennsylvania Assembly and national Congress. At the convention he was a strong nationalist, but he rarely spoke. He died on August 26, 1811.

Benjamin Franklin, 81, called himself simply "philosopher," but earned international fame as a printer, publisher, author, scientist, inventor, and philanthropist. He was the oldest convention delegate and one of the most influential. Franklin suffered from gout and kidney stones, and was too infirm to deliver his own convention speeches; James Wilson read his remarks for him. Franklin rode to and from daily convention sessions in a French sedan chair, carried on the shoulders of four convicts from a local prison. He signed the Declaration of Independence, and at the convention supported a strong national government. He was respected for his wit and intelligence, and his good–natured disposition often served as a damper when others' tempers flared at the convention. On the last day of the proceedings, after the delegates had signed the Constitution, Franklin pointed out to his colleagues a carved replica of the sun on the back of Convention President George Washington's chair. During the months of debate, Franklin said, he often had pondered, but could not determine, the direction of the sun's movement. Now, he added, "I have the happiness to know that it is a rising and not a setting Sun."[1] Benjamin Franklin died on April 17, 1790.

Jared Ingersoll, 38, was a leading Philadelphia lawyer who had graduated from Yale University. At the convention he favored the revision of the Articles of Confederation rather than the construction of a new Constitution. He attended all the sessions but seldom spoke during debates. He ran for U.S. Vice President in 1812, and he died on October 31, 1822.

Thomas Mifflin, 43, was a merchant who had served as quartermaster general for the Revolutionary Army. He was head of the Pennsylvania delegation to the convention, but was overshadowed by his colleagues. He served as Governor of Pennsylvania (1790–1799), and he died on January 20, 1800.

Gouverneur Morris, 35, was a lawyer and a graduate of Columbia University. Though his unusual first name was French, Morris was born in Morrisania, New York. He wore a wooden leg as the result of a carriage accident. Politically influential, he had signed the Articles of Confederation. Morris was a witty and accomplished leader at the convention. He served as a member of the Committee on Postponed Matters and the Committee of Style. He spoke 173 times—more than any other delegate. Morris was minister to France (1792–1794). As a U.S. senator (1800–1803), he supported the Louisiana Purchase. He died on November 6, 1816.

Robert Morris (no relation to Gouverneur Morris), 53, a merchant, was the wealthiest man in Philadelphia, and possibly in America, at the time of the Constitutional Convention. He signed both the Declaration of Independence and the Articles of Confederation. Morris was a leader in the national Congress, and served two terms in the Pennsylvania legislature. He was George Washington's host in Philadelphia, and he nominated Washington as president of the convention. Morris was a U.S. senator in the first U.S. Congress (1789–1795). Later in his life he lost his fortune speculating on western land and served time in debtors' prison. He died, poverty-stricken, on May 8, 1806.

James Wilson, 45, a lawyer born in Scotland, had attended the University of Edinburgh. Eleven years after coming to America, he signed the Declaration of Independence. He was an influential convention delegate. Only Gouverneur Morris spoke more often than James Wilson. He served on the Committee of Detail and supported a strong national government based on the authority of the people. Wilson was an Associate Justice of the U.S. Supreme Court (1789–1798). He died on August 21, 1798.

★ South Carolina

Pierce Butler, 43, a planter, was one of four convention delegates born in Ireland. He served in the South Carolina state legislature and in national Congress. At the convention, Butler served on the Committee on Postponed Matters, and was responsible for the Fugitive Slave clause in the Constitution. He was twice elected to the U.S. Senate (1789–1796 and 1802–1806). Butler died on February 15, 1822.

William Jackson, 28, a businessperson, was born in England, but he came to America at an early age. Though he was elected secretary of the Constitutional Convention, he played a limited role in the proceedings. Since the notes he took were little more than a record of yea and nay votes, the more detailed notes of James Madison and others have proved more valuable to historians. After the convention, Jackson delivered the signed Constitution to the Continental Congress in New York. He ran unsuccessfully for the U.S. Senate in 1789; that same year he was appointed President George Washington's personal secretary. He died on December 18, 1828.

Charles Pinckney, 29, a lawyer, was among the youngest convention delegates and one of the most involved. He had been a member of the national Congress and of his state legislature. As a delegate, he attended all convention sessions and spoke often and effectively. He was responsible for a clause in the Constitution forbidding religious tests as the basis for holding national office. Pinckney later served as a U.S. senator (1799–1801), minister to Spain (1801–1805), and U.S. congressman (1819–1821). He died on October 29, 1824.

Charles Cotesworth Pinckney, 41, Charles Pinckney's cousin, was a lawyer, soldier, and diplomat who attended Christ Church College in Oxford, England. He had served as a general in the Revolutionary Army, and as a state representative (1778 and 1782). He was a key delegate at the convention, supporting a strong national government. In 1796, Pinckney was appointed minister to France. He was a candidate for Vice President in 1800, and he ran for President in 1804 and 1808. He died on August 16, 1825.

John Rutledge, 48, a lawyer, was head of his state's delegation to the Constitutional Convention. He had been governor of South Carolina, and had been a member of both the state assembly and the national Congress. Rutledge served the convention as a member of the Committee of Detail, supporting strong national government. He was appointed as Associate Justice of the U.S. Supreme Court (1789–1791), and died on July 18, 1800.

★ Virginia

John Blair, 55, was a lawyer who had served as Chief Justice of the Virginia Court of Appeals (1780). He took no part in convention debates, but he approved and signed the completed Constitution. He was an Associate Justice of the U.S. Supreme Court (1789–1796). Blair died on August 31, 1800.

James Madison, 36, was a lawyer, a College of New Jersey graduate, and a former member of the national Congress. He had written extensively about the faults of the Articles of Confederation, and he drafted the Virginia Proposal, which was the blueprint for the Constitution. At the convention, Madison served on the Committee on Postponed Matters. After the adjournment of the Constitutional Convention, Madison cowrote *The Federalist Papers* with Alexander Hamilton and John Jay. The articles explained the Constitution and urged its ratification. Later, as a member of the national House of Representatives, Madison was chairman of the committee that wrote the Bill of Rights. James Madison served as the fourth President of the United States. Madison, the last surviving signer of the Constitution, died on June 27, 1836, at the age of 85.

George Washington, 55, was a dignified and respected planter and former commander in chief of the Revolutionary Army. He presided over the convention and therefore did not join in debates. He spoke just twice during the proceedings—once to accept the office of president of the convention, and a second time on the last day of the convention. In 1789, Washington became the first President of the United States, and he was reelected to a second term as President in 1793. Washington died on December 14, 1799, of complications from a sore throat. Physicians at that time bled many patients. Today's opinion is that excessive loss of blood in his already weakened condition probably led to Washington's death.

Appendix B:
Preamble to the Constitution of the United States

We the people of the United States, in order to form a more perfect Union, establish justice, insure domestic tranquility, provide for the common defence, promote the general welfare, and secure the blessings of liberty to ourselves and our posterity, do ordain and establish this Constitution for the United States of America.

Appendix C:
The Bill of Rights

Constitutional amendments I through X, known as the Bill of Rights, were enacted December 15, 1791.

★ Article I

Congress shall make no law respecting an establishment of religion, or prohibiting the free exercise thereof; or abridging the freedom of speech, or of the press; or the right of the people peaceable to assemble, and to petition the Government for a redress of grievances.

★ Article II

A well regulated militia, being necessary to the security of a free State, the right of the people to keep and bear arms shall not be infringed.

★ Article III

No soldier shall, in time of peace be quartered in any house, without the consent of the owner, nor in time of war, but in a manner to be prescribed by law.

★ Article IV

The right of the people to be secure in their persons, houses, papers, and effects, against unreasonable searches and seizures, shall not be violated, and no warrants shall issue, but upon probable cause, supported by oath or affirmation, and particularly describing the place to be searched, and the persons or things to be seized.

★ Article V

No person shall be held to answer for a capital, or otherwise infamous crime, unless on a presentment or indictment of a Grand Jury, except in cases arising in the land or naval forces, or in the militia, when in actual service in time of war or public danger, nor shall any person be subject for the same offence to be twice put in jeopardy of life or limb; nor shall be compelled in any criminal case to be a witness, against himself, nor be deprived of life, liberty, or property, without due process of law; nor shall private property be taken for public use, without just compensation.

★ Article VI

In all criminal prosecutions, the accused shall enjoy the right to a speedy and public trial, by an impartial jury of the State and district wherein the crime shall have been committed, which district shall have been previously ascertained by law, and to be informed of the nature and cause of the accusation; to be confronted with the witnesses against him; to have compulsory process for obtaining witnesses in his favor, and to have the assistance of counsel for his defense.

★ Article VII

In suits at common law, where the value in controversy shall exceed twenty dollars, the right of trial by jury shall be preserved, and no fact tried by a jury, shall be otherwise reexamined in any court of the United States, than according to the rules of the common law.

★ Article VIII

Excessive bail shall not be required, nor excessive fines imposed, nor cruel and unusual punishments inflicted.

★ Article IX

The enumeration in the Constitution, of certain rights, shall not be construed to deny or disparage others retained by the people.

★ Article X

The powers not delegated to the United States by the Constitution, nor prohibited by it to the States, are reserved to the States, respectively, or to the people.

Glossary

American Revolution—(1775–1781). The war for American independence from Great Britain.

Anti–federalists—Those who favored preserving states' rights over rights of a federal government in the debate over ratification of the Constitution.

Articles of Confederation—An agreement among the thirteen original states, approved in 1781. The Articles provided for a weak federal government before the Constitution was enacted in 1789.

bicameral—Having two legislative chambers, or houses.

bill of attainder—Law that allows persons to be arrested and punished, without a court trial.

Bill of Rights—The first ten amendments to the United States Constitution, ratified in 1791.

civil rights—A broad range of privileges, rights, and fundamental personal freedoms guaranteed by the U.S. Constitution, and by subsequent amendments and laws.

colonies—Early American settlements. The original thirteen colonies later became states.

Congress—The two–house legislative body established by the United States Constitution.

Constitutional Convention—The meeting held May 14 to September 17, 1787, in Philadelphia, Pennsylvania, for the purpose of revising or replacing the Articles of Confederation with a new U.S. Constitution.

Declaration of Independence—The document declaring the thirteen American colonies independent from Great Britain, and establishing the United States as a nation, adopted July 4, 1776.

democracy—A system of government run by common people.

electoral college—A group of representatives of the people chosen to elect the President and Vice President of the United States.

electors—Those members of the electoral college chosen to vote for the U.S. President and Vice President.

ex post facto—A law that makes criminal an act that was legal when it was committed.

Federalists—Those who favored a strong national government in the debate over ratification of the U.S. Constitution.

Great Compromise—An agreement reached during the Constitutional Convention about choosing members of Congress. It was credited with saving the convention.

habeas corpus—A legal term meaning that an accused person must be brought before the court with a statement showing sufficient cause for arrest.

impeachment—An accusation of misconduct against a government official.

jurisdiction—The power or right to exercise authority.

legislature—An organized body having the power to make laws.

Magna Carta—Latin for "Great Charter." A list of rights and privileges for English barons, signed under pressure by King John of England in 1215.

national Congress—(also called the Congress of the Confederacy and the Continental Congress). The governing body established by the Articles of Confederation in 1781.

New Jersey Plan—A proposal, submitted during the Constitutional Convention, providing for changes in the Articles of Confederation that would let Congress tax imports and regulate trade, but would also preserve states' rights.

preamble—An introductory statement.

precedent—A court decision that sets a pattern for dealing with future problems.

republic—A system of government run by elected officials representing and responsible to the people.

segregation—The separation or isolation of a group of people, usually by race, class, or ethnic group.

sovereignty—Freedom from external control.

veto—To refuse approval of a bill so that it will be reconsidered or will not be passed.

Virginia Proposal—A proposal, submitted during the Constitutional Convention, resolving to create a government made up of executive, legislative, and judicial branches.

warrant—A document giving legal authority to a police officer to make an arrest or to do other official acts.

Chapter Notes

Chapter I

1. Jeffrey St. John, *Constitutional Journal—A Correspondent's Report From the Convention of 1787* (Ottowa, III: Jameson Books, Inc., 1987), p. 9.

2. Charles L. Mee, Jr., *The Genius of the People* (New York: Harper and Row, 1987), p. 77.

3. St. John, p. 224.

Chapter 2

1. Jethro K. Lieberman, *The Enduring Constitution—A Bicentennial Perspective* (New York: West Publishing Co., 1987), p. 12.

2. Ibid., pp. 21–22.

3. Ibid., p. 22.

4. *The 1994 Information Please Almanac, Atlas, and Yearbook,* 47th edition (Boston and New York: Houghton Mifflin Company, 1994), p. 614.

5. Charles L. Mee, Jr., *The Genius of the People* (New York: Harper and Row, 1987), p. 10.

6. Ralph Mitchell, *CQ's Guide to the U.S. Constitution—History, Text, Glossary, Index* (Washington, D.C.: Congressional Quarterly, Inc., 1986), p. 11.

7. William Peters, *A More Perfect Union—The Making of the United States Constitution* (New York: Crown Publishers, Inc., 1987), p. 81.

8. Ibid., p. 82.

9. Mitchell, p. 9.

10. Jeffrey St. John, *Constitutional Journal—A Correspondent's Report From the Convention of 1787* (Ottowa, III: Jameson Books, Inc., 1987), pp. 214, 215.

Chapter 3

1. Catherine Drinker Bowen, *Miracle at Philadelphia—The Story of the Constitutional Convention, May to September 1787* (Boston: Little, Brown and Co., 1966), frontispiece.

2. Jeffrey St. John, *Constitutional Journal—A Correspondent's Report From the Convention of 1787* (Ottawa, III.: Jameson Books, Inc., 1987), p. 133.

3. Charles L. Mee, Jr., *The Genius of the People* (New York: Harper and Row, 1987), p. 173.

4. Ralph Mitchell, *CQ's Guide to the U.S. Constitution—History, Tat, Glossary, Index* (Washington, D.C.: Congressional Quarterly, Inc., 1986), p. 43.

5. Mee, p. 154.

6. Jethro K. Lieberman, *The Enduring Constitution—A Bicentennial Perspective* (New York: West Publishing Co., 1987), p. 179.

7. Mee, p. 248.

8. Lieberman, p. 324.

Chapter 4

1. Jethro K. Lieberman, *The Enduring Constitution—A Bicentennial Perspective* (New York: West Publishing Co., 1987), p. 155.

2. Ibid., p. 48.

3. Ira Glasser, *Visions of Liberty—The Bill of Rights for All Americans* (New York: Little, Brown and Co., 1991), pp. 38–39.

4. Michael Kammen, ed., *The Origins of the American Constitution—A Documentary History* (New York: Penguin Books, 1986), pp. 255–258.

5. Glasser, pp. 40–41.

6. Edward Oxford, "Documents of Destiny," *American History Illustrated*, January/February 1992, p. 32.

Chapter 5

1. Jethro K. Lieberman, *The Enduring Constitution—A Bicentennial Perspective* (New York: West Publishing Co., 1987), pp. 218–219.

2. Paul Leavitt, "Nationline—Panhandlers Are Free to Beg . . . ," *USA Today, July* 30, 1993, p. 3A.

3. Duane Lockard and Walter F. Murphy, *Basic Cases in Constitutional Law* (Washington, D.C.: Congressional Quarterly Press, 1992), p. 154.

4. Michael D. Simpson, "School Prayer Is Back," *NEA Today,* September 1994, p. 19.

5. LynNell Hancock and Pat Wingert, "Silence in the Classroom," *Newsweek,* October 3, 1994, p. 48.

6. Aric Press, "Tacking Toward Moderation," *Newsweek,* July 11, 1994, p. 58.

7. Ira Glasser, "Visions of Liberty: The Bill of Rights For All Americans" (New York: Little, Brown and Co., 1991), p. 201.

8. Ibid., p. 202.

9. Ibid., p. 171.

10. Editorial, "Warrantless Searches," *USA Today,* April 13, 1994, p. 8A.

11. "Drug Testing," *ABA Journal,* January 1994, pp. 77–78.

12. Ellen Alderman and Caroline Kennedy, *In Our Defense—The Bill of Rights in Action* (New York: William Morrow and Co., Inc., 1991), p. 162.

13. *Facts on File* (New York: Oxford, 1994), p. 276E1.

14. Lockard and Murphy, pp. 282–294.

15. Ibid., pp. 191–203.

Further Reading

Cheney, Lynne. *We the People: The Story of Our Constitution.* New York: Simon & Schuster, 2008.

Taylor-Butler, Christine. *The Constitution of the United States.* New York: Children's Press, 2008.

Sobel, Syl. *The U.S. Constitution and You.* New York: Barron's Educational Series, 2012.

Internet Addresses

Archives.Gov
This Web site offers archived articles and historical information
<http://www.archives.gov/exhibits/charters/constitution.html>

House.Gov
Read the Constitution of the United States on this Web site
<http://www.house.gov/house/Constitution/Constitution.html>

Loc.Gov
Learn about primary documents in American History
<http://www.loc.gov/rr/program/bib/ourdocs/Constitution.html>

Index

A

abortion, 76
accused, rights of, 72–75
amendments to the Constitution,
  51–52
American Civil Liberties Union
  (ACLU), 72
American Revolution, 11, 21, 22,
  50, 61, 61
Annapolis Assembly, 22
Anti–Federalists, 53
archbishop of Canterbury, 16
Article I, 42, 48, 50, 55, 67
Article II, 45, 48
Article III, 56
Article IV, 50
Article VI, 38, 52, 56
Articles of Confederation, 7, 10,
  11, 19, 21, 22, 24, 28, 29, 32,
  42, 48, 50, 52

B

Bank of the United States, 50–51
Bill of Rights, 14, 37, 52, 55–60,
  61, 62, 67, 76
Boston Tea Party, 19

C

civil rights, 67–70
Civil Rights Act of 1964, 69
Committee of Detail, 34, 36, 42, 45
Committee of Style, 36–37, 49

Committee of the Whole, 25,
  29, 31
Committee on Postponed Matters,
  36, 44
Congress of the Confederation, 52
Congress of the United States, 34,
  40, 58
Convention, Constitutional
  adjourned, 14
  agenda, 24–25
  business, 12
  called to order, 8
  clashes, 31–32
  delegate diversity, 10–12

D

Declaration of Independence, 8,
  11, 21, 62
double jeopardy, 73
drug testing, 72

E

electoral college, 36, 45
electors, 36, 38, 45, 49
Equal Rights Amendment (ERA),
  51–52
executive branch, 42–45
ex post facto laws, 51, 56

F

Federalist Papers, 53
Federalists, 53, 58

First Amendment, 61–67
First Continental Congress, 21
flag–burning, 64
Fourteenth Amendment, 60, 67, 69
Franklin, Benjamin, 8, 10, 11, 38, 86
freedom of religion, 62, 64, 66–67
freedom of the press, 61–62, 64

G
Great Compromise, The, 32–33

H
habeas corpus, 55–56
Hamilton, Alexander, 10, 22, 31, 37, 42, 44, 53, 84

J
Jefferson, Thomas, 7, 12, 45, 57, 58
Jim Crow laws, 69
Jones v. Clear Creek Independent School District, 66
judicial branch, 45–48

K
King John, 16, 18
King, Martin Luther, Jr., 71
King Richard, 16
King, Rodney, 73
Kiryas Joel v. Grumet, 66–67

L
Lafayette, Marquis de, 14, 41
Lee v. Weisman, 66
legal tender, 50
legislative branch, 41–42

M
Madison, James, 7, 10, 12, 22, 25, 29, 36, 37, 45, 59, 53, 57, 58, 60, 89
Magna Carta, 16–18
Massachusetts Bay Charter, 19
Mayflower Compact, 18
Miranda v. Arizona, 74, 75

N
national executive, 27, 31, 42
New Jersey Plan, 28–29, 42

P
panhandling, 64
Pennsylvania State House, 8, 9, 13
Philadelphia, Pennsylvania, 21, 24
Plessy v. Ferguson, 69
Preamble to the Constitution, 90
President, 34, 36, 42–45, 46, 47
punishment, cruel and unusual, 75

R
ratification of Constitution, 37, 38, 52–54, 58
religious tests, 52, 56
roadblock searches, 70, 72
Roe v. Wade, 76

S
school prayer, 64, 66–67
seditious libel, 62
Shays' Rebellion, 24
signers of Constitution, 79–89
signing of Constitution, 38, 39
slavery, 49–50
Stamp Act Congress, 19

Stamp Act of 1765, 19
State of the Union Address, 47
states, power of, 50–51
states' rights, 10, 47
Supremacy Clause, 48
Supreme Court, 46, 47, 48, 64,
    66, 67, 69, 70, 72, 75, 76

T
Thirteenth Amendment, 50, 69
three–fifths ratio, 33, 49
two–thirds vote, 48–49

U
United States v. Eichman, 64
University of Colorado v. Derdeyn,
    72

V
Virginia Proposal, 25–27, 28, 29,
    31, 42, 45
voting, 67–70

W
Washington, George, 8, 10, 11,
    14, 15, 21, 25, 26, 31, 41, 45,
    49, 50, 89

Z
Zenger, John Peter, 62